1 MONTH OF FREE READING

at

www.ForgottenBooks.com

By purchasing this book you are eligible for one month membership to ForgottenBooks.com, giving you unlimited access to our entire collection of over 700,000 titles via our web site and mobile apps.

To claim your free month visit:
www.forgottenbooks.com/free236882

* Offer is valid for 45 days from date of purchase. Terms and conditions apply.

ISBN 978-0-483-36601-5
PIBN 10236882

This book is a reproduction of an important historical work. Forgotten Books uses state-of-the-art technology to digitally reconstruct the work, preserving the original format whilst repairing imperfections present in the aged copy. In rare cases, an imperfection in the original, such as a blemish or missing page, may be replicated in our edition. We do, however, repair the vast majority of imperfections successfully; any imperfections that remain are intentionally left to preserve the state of such historical works.

Forgotten Books is a registered trademark of FB &c Ltd.
Copyright © 2017 FB &c Ltd.
FB &c Ltd, Dalton House, 60 Windsor Avenue, London, SW19 2RR.
Company number 08720141. Registered in England and Wales.

For support please visit www.forgottenbooks.com

The Maid of Lipara

The figure that you here see put
Was for H. Buxton Forman cut;
Amid his household gods to bide
And relics culled from far and wide.
This book is his on whom you look;
For Scott his graving tackle took

And etched the man to watch therein,
That none by guile the book might win.
Then siste fur! of great and small
The world holds books enough for all.
Of roughly handling this beware,
And put it in its place with care!

1875

HARVARD COLLEGE LIBRARY
DEXTER FUND

The Maid of Lipara.

WHERE Æolus, King of Storms, had earlier reign'd,
That shining island of the Tyrrhene Sea,
Of rocky aspect, in whose caverns deep
He stored the winds, and bade the tempests stay;—
That island where the faint volcano-glare
Sheds, nightly seen, from sources confluent—
In the arcana of the earth, profound,—
With Ætna's seething pit—abode of fire!
Where Mulciber, with Cyclops hammering toil'd,—
Circled in ardent and sulphureous flames—
At anvils, for the thunderbolts of Jove!
Ay, Lipara! there dwelt a daintie maid,
Constantia named; of noble ancestry,
Tenderly nurtured in the lap of ease,—

THE MAID OF LIPARA.

For since the gods were gone, and Lipara's fires
Blazed upwards, but to lighten, not to scathe,
The isle grew plenteous for the wants of men.
That time was when the turban'd Saracen
Held with the Christian a divided sway;—
A simpler age, of thought more fresh and free,
When hearts were hearts, and love a love
    undoubting,
And when emotion had its pristine play.
The maid show'd beauty passing common praise—
As though an angel had her mother met!
Oval, mild-melting, silken-fringéd eyes,
Whose placid sheen, as of a glassy lake,
Betoken'd depths profound, and purity,—
Whate'er the mood, true beacons of her soul;—
Slender yet strong, and agile as the roe,
And rounded as the Phidian master-piece;
Luxuriant tresses, mantling o'er a brow
Whereon it seem'd the sun, unsetting, shined,—
The pride of Lipara,—but none her own!
Constantia reach'd the age contemplative,—
Not all the present,—when a future dawns,
A land of promise, and illusions sweet!
Ere then a child, of brightest children one,
She had been joyant, and brim-full of love;
She loved her kin, and all of human kind,
Her doll, gazelle, and petted dogs and doves,
She kiss'd the flowerets, with endearing words,

THE MAID OF LIPARA.

And took delight in butterfly or bee.
She loved the moon, the stars, sea, earth, or sky,—
The humpéd camel, or the graceful horse,
The pretty babe, or squalid beggar bare,
And, of the wrinkled toad, but saw its eye.
She had been happy, as the roses are!
Drinking the dew-drop, paying back perfume,—
But now there came a void within her heart;
The loves she loved were not enough to love,
Neither enough for her, to be beloved.
Her mother loved her fondly,—not enough!
She must have love in love,—herself, alone.

    At Lipara they held high festival
To vaunt the birthday of the Æolian king,
Whereat went forth the island chivalry,
In holiday trim, and warlike pageantry,
For games athletic, and the frolic joust.
Constantia, with her kindred, forward placed,
In simple-hearted, girlish merriment,
Bred by the changeful motions of the hour,—
Forgat the hungering void, and look'd, and laugh'd,
As one uncaring, save to be amused.
Then, in the final joust, the victor proven
Had for his praise the circus to pass round,
And yield the guerdon to the fairest fair—
Martucci Gomito,—reining a milk-white barb
Of purest Arab blood, and proudest pace.

Constantia mark'd him distant—his fierce eye,
Broad forehead, clustering hair, and manly form,
And, in that moment,—knew the void was filled!
As one spell-bound, she gazed, whilst on he came,
Bowing and scanning as he moved along,
The myrtle wreath in hand, prepared to throw.
And still, spell-bound, she gazed, she knew not
    why,
To see him cast the guerdon,—till now near,
His steed, by fright, or by his heel compell'd,
Rear'd and curvetted,—to the fear of most,—
Whilst she, unscared, yet gazing, saw him bend
Low, to the girths,—the chaplet on her lap!
Up to his eyes she look'd,—Martucci look'd,
And saw the tinctures of her heart suffuse
Her delicate cheek—the primogenial blush!
Sprung from its sources for Martucci's sake,
The efflorescence of her maidenhood!
And then her craving soul was satisfied.

    Erelong, as lover, brave Martucci came
To her paternal home, and ardently
Preferr'd his claim, as victor, for the maid
To whom he gave the guerdon,—fairest fair!
They said, "He was not noble, was not mate
For a companion of their royal race,
Nor wealth enough had he to wed with her."
Constantia pleaded, "He is my first love,

THE MAID OF LIPARA.

My only love, for him I live or die;
Oh! mother, let me love him—for I muſt."

Martucci, raging, ſaid, "I'll make me noble,
The wealth will live to gain, or, failing, periſh!"
And ſo he raſhly ſped, with galliots twain,
To ſcour the ſeas, and ſpoil the Saracen.
Boldly he ventured, and his fame came back:
" Rich prizes from the infidel had won,
And would bring home an argoſy of gold."

The while Conſtantia languiſh'd, in fond hopes,—
Dreaming one dream, awaking ſtill to dream,
Neglecting much her pets and playful taſks,
For now her loves concentrated in one.

But bold Martucci overſtrain'd his aim!
And, by a day, too long delay'd return.
The Saracen in double ſtrength came forth,
His convoy intercepted, and o'ercame,
And, with him, took it to the Afric ſhore.

The triſtful tidings faſt to Lipara flew;—
The maiden heard but this—" Martucci dead!"

Then was love dead to ſweet Conſtantia!
She moved in light unwitting of the light;
The ſtars were cruel, and the moon but ſad,

THE MAID OF LIPARA.

The sunshine did not warm, the earth a blank
Of all affections, creatures, colours all.
The fabric had its lovely form preserved,
Albeit the ghostly habitants were gone!
She could not weep because there were no tears
Left in the outshed fountains of her heart.
Weary with weariness no rest could cure,
She wander'd hither, thither, as in dark,
Her beauteous eyes wide open, day or night.

And yet the world wags on its wonted way;
The portals open'd, revellers came and went.
One night, Constantia, soul-sick utterly,
Covering her head in the mantilla fold,
Mix'd with the parting guests, among them forth!
Out, out she glided, thinking, dolefully,
" I have no home, for me the wide, wide world;
Night is as day, and day to me as night,
Let Nature do with me as Nature will."
And on she flitted through the sinuous streets,
Narrow, obscure and steep, and stony-rough,
Until she knew the dawn; and, as the sun
Uprose, she saw the strand, and out beyond
The sea,—and, on the strand, a fisher's skiff,
Made ready for the labours of the day.

With automatic skill, she loosed the boat,
Unshipp'd the rudder, threw adrift the oars,

And push'd away. The wind blew off the
    shore,
The sail was set, and bore its burthen on,—
The freight a thinking, dormant chrysalid,—
To the dread hazard of the waters wild.

Constantia knew it all,—not wisely knew,
But as synthetic with her fantasies;
And thus far, happy was she,—for she said,
" Am I not desolate,—withouten hope,
So whither in the finite can I go?
If earth to me is nought, there is the sea,
And it may bear me to Martucci's soul."
Along the boat, recumbent, looking to
The sky, by this time brightening into day,
She had one thought alone,—that thought,—Martucci.
She saw, by fancy pictured, his first smile
When he bestowed the guerdon; his hot look
Of scorn, of anger, of frustrated love,
When he was deemed unworthy; his wide chest
Heaving with furious storm, and all for her!
Heroic features cast in Grecian mould,
Shoulders Herculean touch'd by curly locks,
His stature that rear'd upwards, like a god;
And, in the ecstasy, her grief forgot.

Apace the skiff is wandering with the wind.

The moon has mounted, and the ſtars ſhine out.
Conſtantia, with her ever-open eyes,
Stars unto ſtars! beheld them, unſurpriſed,
Thinking they look'd, and ſpake, and lighted
    her.
As a pure ſoul, ſoaring in æther clear,—
A dream upon the ocean floated ſhe!
A pearl ſo perfected, ſo dear to heaven,
A miracle was granted for her ſake,—
Two ſeraphs hovering o'er the fragile ark,
Fanning its puny canvas volantly.

   The hours depart uncounted, and the maid
Lapſing, unnouriſh'd, faint, and comatoſe,
Fell into trance,—tranſlated inſtantly!
She, with her loved Martucci, lived in heaven,
He to an angel changed, with ſapphire wings;—
Upon his breaſt her head, his eyes to hers.
She ſaid, "My love, I've come to thee ſomeway,
And much rejoice to find thee anywhere!"
She heard the muſic heard amid the ſpheres,
And knew its meaning,—ſpeaking to her thus,—

      "*Doubt not, Conſtantia,*
        Love does not die,
      Thy love is reckoned
        In thy ſofteſt ſigh.

> "*Doubt not, Constantia,*
> *Thy love is dear*
> *To the blest angels*
> *Ever, ever here.*
>
> "*Doubt not, Constantia,*
> *As mortal, blind,*
> *Be thou but constant,*
> *Thou thy love shalt find.*
>
> "*Doubt not, Constantia,*
> *If grieved thy life,*
> *Be thou still constant,*
> *Yet wilt thou be wife.*"

Supernal strains yet sounding in her soul,
Constantia felt a soft encircling arm
Her from her hapless resting-place remove;—
Stranded the miracle-boat in little bay
Nigh Syrtis Minor gulph.

". What are you, dear ?
Whence came you, pretty child ?" spake Carapresa,
Fondling the wondrous waif maternally,—
For Carapresa was of Christian race
Of Trapáni native, and by garb she knew
The damsel must have drifted from afar.
At break of morn she came to meet the fishers,

On whom, as slave, she waited. "Pretty dear!
Speak, for thy language is, I think, as mine."
Constantia, looking into space some while,
Moan'd out at last, "I know not—leave me here."
Then Carapresa, grown compassionate,
Bore the submissive maid with haste unto
The shelter of her cabin, there outstretch'd
Upon the scant bed laid her, sitting by,
Admired her gazing eyes, much wondering
To see such beauty in such wretchedness;
Gave her some simple food, as nurse would do
To infant,—silent watch'd and watch'd until
The bright orbs closed, and sweet Constantia slept.
A long, long sleep! Long Carapresa watch'd
To see those eyes re-open, for she thought
"Perchance it endeth in the sleep of death."
The angels came about the couch and smiled
On wizen'd Carapresa, waiting there,—
For though she saw them not, she knew they smiled.
As the night wanderer notes the streak of morn,
So that poor watcher saw the fringéd lids
Uplift to light and life; rejoicing greatly;—
"Sweet, pretty pet, I welcome thee anew,
Thou hast been slumbering, and I wished thee
    wake."
Constantia, as in vision, with no sight,—
"Where am I now, and who art thou so kind?"
"Thou art near Susa, of the Afric land,

Poor Caraprefa I."—Then raifing her,
She laved her gently, comb'd her flowing hair,
Chafed her white, velvet hands, and tiny feet,
Carefully clothed her, muttering timoroufly,
" She is a princefs—whence fuch lovelinefs?
She is an angel, fair and beautiful,
What fhall I do to guard her from reproach,—
Save her from infidel clutch, and luftful look?"
Then turn'd her thoughts to heaven for help and
    light.
Continuing,—" Now know I what to do,—
To good Alathiel take her,—if fhe will."

    Alathiel, a fair Moflem dame high-born,
Wealthy, life-wearied by a broken love.
Retired to Sufa, fhe had there devifed
Afylum merciful for maidens meek,
Guiding the effluent energies of youth
In ways of virtue, and induftrious arts,—
A quiet, calm feclufion, where no man
Muft dare to enter.

                Caraprefa faid,
Mumbling her reverie, as beldams do;—
" Left fhe fhould flee,—I'll keep her as a bird
(The bird this Peri, and my hut the cage)."
So Caraprefa, comforting the maid
With fuch fparfe fuccours as the pooreft have,

Went out to reckon with her masters rough,—
Locking her door, screening the window, close,—
And came again at eventide, and found
Constantia sitting, tranquil and forlorn,
Her splendent eyes wide-looking to no-where,—
And said, "My dear, wilt thou not with me go?"
"Having no home, shall I not wend with thee?—
Having no home, my home is anywhere."
Then, in the stillness of the murky night,
The fishers gone to sea, the land at hush,
Kind Caraprefa wrapp'd her, led her out,
And, oft supporting, somewhiles carrying her,
Help'd by a market-cart that sought the town,—
To Sufa* brought her,—to Alathiel's haven ;—
Sufa a city opulent and gay,
With frowning fortress on a craggy steep,—
Across that shore where Titan Atlas lifts,
Transformed to mountain vast, his mighty back,—
Doom'd to uphold the firmamental sphere.

It was the early hour when sleep with most
Is weak, or over, and when cries and raps
Are heard, but fright not ; so Alathiel heard,
Observing that the hour was break of day,
Saying to her maidens, "Fear not, I'll descend."
Soon, through the lattice-bars, in grey-eyed light,

---

* Ancient Adrumetum.

Alathiel scann'd the matron and the maid,
Gave patient ear to Carapresa's pleading,
Then, moving bolts and bars, with tremulous hand
Open'd the jealous door, and bade them in.

And when Alathiel mark'd the scaréd eyes
Of lost Constantia, watch'd her 'witching ways,
Heard her weird words of woe,—unblaming any—
Noted her beauty, and her air of grace,—
Learning the most of the romantic tale—
She added love to chasten'd charity
Towards the strange sea-waif, and nestled her,
To soothe her, night or day, with comfortings;
Saying to the maidens, " Give her tender speech,
And solace her in aught she hath to do."
For when Alathiel asked her whence she came,
She only said, " I know not, I'm Constantia ;
There was a world I lived in, but 'tis gone;
The people in it were both good and cruel,
And now 'tis past, I know not where I am."

Constantia with the maidens sate, their queen,
In virtue of her saintly influence,
E'en as its fragrance makes us bless the flower;—
She had a charm upon her, from the skies,
Surpassing reason, having reason none;
The favourite of a benignant star,
She, by a look, could warm the frigid heart

And quicken it to impulse; she would work
Among the diligent sisters silently,
Yet with the art to win their reverence;
Embroider'd well, and wove the endless web,
And plaintive ditties warbled to the moon.
Listening their gossip, she so smiled and gazed,—
They read it for the language of the soul.
She had their love, in love with no restraint,
But in some awe of her, as heaven-born.

Just then the King of Tunis and that land,—
The sage and prudent Mariabdela,—
By a Granadan prince was hardly press'd,
On a disputed title to his throne.
Martucci Gomito, a captive, pined
At Tunis; he had heard the news, and thought
A thought that, acted, promised liberty.
He by the warders being favour'd there,
As one of gracious manners, noble traits,
Said to his gaoler—"Let me see your chief."
Then to the master boldly he outspoke,
"I pray that you do take me to the King;
Tell that the stratagem I would propose
Shall, by adoption, give him victory."
The master bore that message, and eftsoons
Into the royal presence render'd him.
"I thank thee for this gift of grace, O King!
Would crave thine hearing to my stratagem."

The King,—" Proceed, we have our ears to hear."
" Thou counteſt on thine archers,—ſo thy foe;
And more, they argue that, their arrows flown,
Yours will they have to follow;—order then,
With utmoſt privity to lateſt hour,
More fine than theirs, your bowſtrings to be made,
Your arrow-ſlits the ſame,—to fit the ſtring;
Refrain, whilſt they, elate, their quivers void,
Then, like a hailſtorm pelting, looſe your ſhafts!
Soon will they find your narrow-mouthéd darts
Refuſe their bowſtrings—whilſt your archers ſhoot,
Doubly ſupplied, their arrows in return:
A panic in their hearts ſurpriſe ſhall breed,
Then, royal ſir, thou haſt but to purſue."
" 'Tis well," quoth Mariabdela,—" ſee thou to it!
And, at the battle, ſtand thou by my ſide.
If victory follow, I will ſay 'tis thine,
Thou ſhalt high honour have, and rich reward."
Martucci formed the archery to his faſhion;—
The battle went as, ſhrewdly, he forecaſt,
King Mariabdela his foe repulſed
With ſlaughter great, and with diſperſion wide.

Donna Alathiel, owning lands at Tunis,
Was thither ſummon'd, to protect her rights.
Alathiel loved Conſtantia,—ponder'd thus;—
" She is a graceful ſtatue, it were well
To wake it up,—to bring it back to life

By fights and founds of ftimulant verities;—
Recall her memory to things that were,
By ftreets and marts, and fprightly circumftance
Occurring in the genial haunts of men."
" Dear fofter-child, I now to Tunis part;
There fpeed thou with me, that fair city fee."
" Mother, I care not, care not whither where—
Only with thee for ever would I reft."
Together went they unto Tunis' city,
Halting betimes at houfe and hoftelrie,
(Whereat the dame, foreknown, warm welcome
    found,)
And, as they wended, thofe the maid beheld
Thought her divine, and bleff'd her on her way.
Coming to Tunis as the combat ended,—
For little then was known of diftant things,—
Alathiel heard that prefently would be
A royal pomp of triumph national.

    The ftreets bedizen'd were in rainbow hues,
That the fantaftic Saracen fancy charm;
The people buoyant in their late reprieve
From the invader's grafp, and in their pride
Of victory, jubilant with dance and fong.
Conftantia look'd, and look'd, but fmiléd never;
Her ever brilliant eyes gazed onward ever,—
Not one fide, nor the other; what fhe heard
None knew by hearing,—for fhe did not fpeak.

She breathed as others breathe; and yet the air
Gave not her pulfes purpofes of life.
The while, endow'd with art mechanical,
Her fingers deft the loom would nimbly ply
Or with entrancing pathos touch the lyre;
She trod the earth as one of other fphere,
Whofe thoughts and language are to men unknown.
She look'd up to the fun, but faw no fun,—
As 'twere what mortals fee was not to her.

It is the day of triumph, and the King
With our Martucci the proceffion led;
He had the Liparæan thus proclaim'd,—
" This noble youth hath Mariabdela faved;
Let him henceforth be honour'd of you all."
After the King rode minifters and peers,
In glittering trappings, blazon'd gorgeoufly,
Then captives, and the trophies of the fpoil.

Alathiel, of patrician rank, was grouped
With noble ladies of the King and court,
Conftantia by her, as the Moflems, veil'd.
They faw the Triumph moving from afar
To the wide area of the palace (bright
With gilded domes, and minarets painted o'er),
Where they were fitting,—for the king had faid
There, at the clofe, he would the victor crown.

Fronting Alathiel's tent the Triumph stay'd;
Martucci Gomito, his visor down,
Riding the prime companion of the King:
Alighting there, the King Martucci brought
Near to the tent, the victor's wreath upheld,
Lifted his visor, next his helmet raised,
Bestow'd the laurel, with loud voice pronouncing,
"Lo! crown for crown, this crown a king doth
  yield."

Then, through the tent and the surrounding host,
Was heard a cry of joy ineffable!
Only one word, "Martucci!"—Quick, unveil'd,
Constantia, springing from Alathiel's side,
Leap'd to Martucci's neck, and on him hung,—
Saying, "Martucci!—I have found my love."
Martucci whisper'd,—"Yea, in me thy love!"
The King advanced, unruffled, and releasing,
Surrender'd her to dame Alathiel's arms:
"We will to-morrow speak of her to thee."

Those ever-gazing eyes now gazed to see,—
With her Martucci seeing—two in one!—
To right or left, above, beneath, around.
Constantia hail'd the sunshine with delight,
Saw banners fluttering in the lively breeze,
Saw soldiers, horses, and the pageantry;
Saw the prismatic colours of costumes,

The palace fair,—and heard the clarion ring,
Heard women's voices (of all music most!)
And oh! she knew of sights and sounds most dear,—
After that waking vision of Martucci,—
The lineaments now vocal of Alathiel.
In her first hour of joy she had outsaid
All Carapresa wot not of,—and next,
"Dear mother, more than mother! I awoke
To see thy face, to see thee with my mind,
To know what thou hast done, by grace of God,
For a poor, luckless, strange, demented thing—
My debt too great to reckon in this world!"
Alathiel clasp'd her, kiss'd away her tears,
Saying "Sweet child,—it was by grace of God."

Henceforth the loves long frozen in her soul
Well'd like a fount-spring suddenly set free.
She praised the sun, extoll'd the bountiful earth,
And her thanksgiving eyes to God upraised.
Alathiel for her cared unceasingly,
And spake to her as mother to her child.
"God hath not, dear Constantia, given to me
A child of earth, but thee hast sent, of heaven,
That I should know in thee maternal love.
It is an act of His beneficence,
That thou, not mortal of my body born,
Art as the very offspring of my soul.

Have I not foster'd thee with mother's milk
Of kindness,—fed thee like a cradled babe,
When by misfortune thou wert babe again?"
"Yea, mother! it is so, and thou indeed
Art as the author of my new-born mind.
(Oh! first, own mother! thee I ever love
Although thou hadst no pity for my tears).
Am I not doubly blest in loving thee
With love scarce lesser than my deepest love?
For I have learn'd, by grief, that, lacking love,
Whate'er the gifts, this world is dark and
    drear,—
A barren wilderness—nor sight nor sound!
Withouten love, no glories in the sky,
Withouten love, no music in the air,
Withouten love, no blossoms on the mead."

    The King had pride in sweet Constantia—
Esteem'd her as a jewel to his crown,
And even as a daughter to his heart.
Yet being told the marvellous history,—
Knowing Martucci would the maiden wed,
And, wedded, to his native land repair,
Released him, as or friend or prisoner,
Dower'd him with wealth, and titles adequate,
And gave his nuptials royal countenance.

    Martucci to Alathiel homage tender'd.

One hand to her, and to Constantia one,
Standing between, he said, "I love you both;—
Shall not I love the saviour of my love?
Donna Alathiel, wilt thou with us dwell?"
Alathiel answer'd, "Saracen am I!
But can I part from her, my single child,
Sent me by Heaven, whereto my duty flows?
Yea, I will go! for, whatsoe'er the wrench,
Is nought to loss of my celestial boon."

A day of mourning was it when they went.
The King much sorrowful,—the people sad
To lose their champion and miraculous maid.
For transport safe, the King his best ship lent.
Alathiel, Carapresa, and the pair,
Quitted the port, 'mid tears and blessings rife;
Æolus favour'd, and Constantia fair
To Lipara return'd,—Martucci's wife.

CPSIA information can be obtained
at www.ICGtesting.com
Printed in the USA
BVHW040538101118
532319BV00026B/2005/P